INTEND

A man's heart plans his way,
but the LORD directs his steps.

Proverbs 16:9

(NKJV)

DR. JONATHAN C. CAREY

CAREY PRESS
EQUIPPING ENCOURAGING EMPOWERING

INSPIRE SERIES: Intend

Copyright © 2018 Jonathan C. Carey

All rights reserved under International and Pan-American Copyright Conventions

No part of this book may be reproduced, stored in a retrieval system or transmitted in any way by any means, electronic, mechanical, photocopy, recording or otherwise without the prior permission of the author except as provided by USA copyright law.

All Scripture quotations are taken from the Authorized King James Version of the Bible.

Published by Carey Press
http://www.careypress.online
Published in the United States of America

ISBN-13: 978-1717110114

Contents

This Series Is Dedicated to the Bahamas and Caribbean Provincial Leaders of Global United Fellowship

Preface

This series was developed to provide, in workbook form, concepts for personal and leadership success. It targets two groups. First, men and women who are in leadership positions globally, as a leadership and life-coaching tool. Second, believers who seek biblically-based personal-development study materials.

The concepts are taken from biblical characters, reflecting part of their life's quest and challenges. I hope the series will be welcomed not only by leaders and believers for life-coaching/personal study, but also by Bible training institutes, mission organizations, Sunday school classes, cell groups, prison ministries, and all those who are involved in the maturing of the saints. The author is available, on a limited basis, to conduct INSPIRE-related workshops and seminars.

Biblical Perspective

Successful personal-ministry developmental concepts flow from the pages of the Bible, but are these concepts applicable for believers today? Indeed they are. What then are we to do with these biblical concepts to success? Perhaps the first step is the creation-maintenance of an environment in our ministries and organizations where they are recognized, taught, and encouraged.

Biblical-related success occurs when believers respond in obedience to God's call. They recognize the importance of total obedience, allowing the Holy Spirit to develop their gifts and skills. They carry out their kingdom roles with a deep conviction of God's will and a heightened awareness of the contemporary issues they and their peers face. Above all, they minister as stewards and servants.

We do not stumble across success. Success is a result of deliberate acts. To truly be successful, we must fulfil the will of God for our lives!

The Bible teaches that we can be successful only when we are in right relationship with God. This right relationship is made possible by the death and resurrection of the Lord Jesus Christ. May we always INTEND on allowing the Lord to direct our steps.

Introduction

On a dry September night, unbeknown to me, the setting for the concepts shared here was coming into focus.

September 7, 2017 was not only my birthday, but also the anxious days and moments before the expected arrival of Hurricane Irma on September 9. As I sat quietly trying to decide on what direction I would take in regards to the approaching hurricane, I heard the Spirit speak to me and ask what appeared to be a simple question. The question was "*Why was Sodom and Gomorrah destroyed?*"

This question rang louder than all the hurricane-related thoughts swirling around in my head. My answer was quick. "*Because of their sin, they were destroyed.*" Immediately, I knew there was more the Spirit was communicating. Upon reflection, I realized the Lord impressed upon me a course of action through a question format. The course of action was clear. The church as the righteous of the city must *pray, plan, and be purposeful* in its collective efforts. Obedience would be our responsibility and outcomes God's.

As we called a group of men together for prayer and planning, we sensed the favour of the Lord upon our lives, and amazedly the forecast of fifteen-foot waves no longer seemed daunting.

Key West, Florida has, as every city does, its unique challenges and opportunities. We are located at mile marker zero in the southernmost part of the United States. Getting to us is not as much of a challenge as leaving when there are mandatory evacuations. Despite these and other challenges, we still enjoy a flourishing tourist-related economy. However, any natural disaster, regardless of its magnitude, threatens our enjoyed way of life.

I have learned throughout the years that hidden in every crisis are opportunities for adding value to a community and advancing the Kingdom of God. These opportunities have to be unpacked and embraced. I knew I would stay during the hurricane not to "*ride out the storm*," but to engage the community and witness the compassion of Christ for all. Engage we did.

What started out as an undersized team using what was collectively in its hands, grew into a response partnership with compassion-focused organizations. We are eternally grateful to the Billy Graham Association, Convoy of Hope, Global United Fellowship, and Samaritan's Purse for not only their partnership, but for leading the way in engaging our communities with passion and compassion. In these community efforts, Samaritan's Purse was our *lead-ship*.

I am also appreciative to Bishop Neil C. Ellis, Presiding Bishop of Global United Fellowship, for his visionary leadership and his ability to sense the direction of the Spirit for the church. It is these qualities that in part motivated the writing of this workbook.

THE INSPIRE SERIES presents seven concepts (Intend, Negotiate, Sanctify, Pray, Influence, Relate, and Engage) derived from the acronym INSPIRE and represent one result of our interaction with Hurricane Irma, our community, faith partners, and the Holy Spirit. Study the concepts in their order because each one builds on the previous. If you step ahead, you will miss the intended impact. This workbook takes a closer look at the verb Intend.

The study format is consistent throughout. The method of study is derived from the acronym STEPS.

THE CITY OF KEY WEST
P.O. BOX 1409
KEY WEST, FL 33041-1409

Craig Cates
Mayor

1300 White Street
(305) 809-3840
ccates@keywestcity.com

November 17, 2017

Dear Pastor Carey and the members of Glad Tidings Tabernacle,

Thank you for everything you have done for the City of Key West. When Hurricane Irma hit our island in September, even though you too had gone through the devastation, you did not hesitate to step up and help our people. When supplies and assistance started pouring in, you immediately offered your services to get our citizens what they needed. You reached out and served as one of the very first hubs for distribution of goods to the city. Thank you for your selfless acts of kindness.

I said in the beginning that when all of the outside agencies leave, and people continue to need help, the church will still be there. You are a pillar of the community and you have proven time and time again that we can count on you to help us get through any challenge we might face.

Thank you for coordinating the tremendous efforts of recovery. It has been a humbling experience to work across the street and witness firsthand what you and your team does on a daily basis to ensure that our citizens have hope and help. We are so grateful to call you a friend and neighbor.

May God continue to bless you all for the good work that you do.

Sincerely,

Craig Cates

Mayor Craig Cates
City of Key West

Key to the Caribbean – Average yearly temperature 77° F.

6

STEPS

State the Step
Teach the Step
Evaluate the Step
Practice the Step
See the Success

PART ONE

INSPIRE SERIES

Intend

Having a Plan or Purpose

State the Step

Every step God takes toward us is done on purpose for a purpose. He is an Intentional God in Creation.

Teach the Step

Intend on Creating

INTEND ON CREATING

*And God said, Let us make man in our image, after our
likeness: and let them have dominion over the fish of the
sea, and over the fowl of the air, and over the cattle, and
over all the earth, and over every creeping thing that
creepeth upon the earth. So God created man in his own
image, in the image of God created he him; male and
female created he them. And God blessed them, and God
said unto them, Be fruitful, and multiply, and replenish
the earth, and subdue it: and have dominion over the
fish of the sea, and over the fowl of the air, and over
every living thing that moveth upon the earth.*

(Genesis 1:26-28)

The day I first meet Shena's mother was punctuated with
an awkward moment. The first question her mother asked
was *"What is your intention with my only child?* I was so
nervous that all I remember saying was a single word "happy."
Apparently I said more because I was given the go ahead to
date Shena.

The older I become, the more intentional are my steps,
whether it's a simple outing with the grandchildren, climb-
ing one of our mountain ministry locations, or planning a
board meeting. I'm intentional not only because of the aging process, but more so because of my desire to add value

13

to others and experience godly outcomes. We should not have to experience the aging process to live intentional lives, or become intentional in our relationships, businesses, or ministries. Intentional steps should be grafted into our psyche because of the revelation or illumination received from hearing, observing, and obeying an intentional God.

The very first book of the Bible records numerous intentional acts by God. From creation to redemption, we observe the triune God-Head acting intentionally.

Let us now take a closer look at the creation of mankind by God. He created us so we may fulfil His purpose for our lives, which in part is living intentionally in His name, power, and for His Glory.

Mankind was created in the image and likeness of God not by chance or an afterthought. Creation was intentional and in that creation thought and act was a built-in redemption plan (Genesis 1:26-28).

It is not paranoia to anticipate problems and have a predetermined course of action. It is wise to have a well-thought-out plan for maintaining the integrity of what you have created. Often that plan must account for how to return your creation to its original intent and direction if required. We will further discuss this in the next chapter.

Made in His image and likeness

We were made in the likeness of God, and because of this we ought to reflect in thought and deed the nature of our Creator God. We should be as intentional toward others as

14

God was toward Adam and Eve. We represent His likeness and must display His love and goodwill toward mankind.

We must be intentional in mirroring His attributes, and one of those attributes is an unconditional love for and toward His creation. As leaders, we understand this, as we nurture and guide the organizations birthed by the Holy Spirit. Going deeper, we must develop the same love for others. Why were we made this way? Here are a few thoughts:

So God can fellowship with us - God desires fellowship

We were created with the aptitude and longing to have fellowship with God. It is spiritually natural, and those out of fellowship with their Creator must be told that the longing they have is really for fellowship with their God. It is part of their DNA.

We as Believers ought to honour our relationship with God by the way we obey Him and manage everything He has entrusted to us. Our honouring should never be an afterthought, but rather at the forefront of our thinking process. Let us always be committed to maximizing our God-given likeness in our fellowship with God and others. Everything we ever wish to accomplish stems from the foundation of fellowship with our Creator. Jesus Christ the only begotten Son of God is said to have stated these sentiments in John 5:19-20.

So God can equip us - Communicate godly knowledge

It was not God's intent for Adam and Eve to know the difference between good and evil, or at least in this juncture of their relationship with their Creator (Genesis 2:17). Their complete knowledge base was to be given to them through communication with God. This is an interesting thought. We do not have to be intimately acquainted with knowledge of evil to be successful as Believers and ministers. Truth needs no comparisons.

What is also interesting in the account of Genesis 2:17-18 is that it appears God told Adam before Eve was created His wishes concerning the tree of the knowledge of good and evil. On a side note, did Adam adequately communicate this information to Eve? As leaders, effective communication skills are a must for success. Communication is not just in what is said, but also in how it is received and understood by the hearer.

Often in our assemblies we have a testimony time. This time allotted allows individuals to share victories secured in their personal lives by the grace of God. Most of the testimonies revolve around how God delivered them from some form of addiction or negative behaviour. At one of these services, Shena whispered to me, "*But I have never experienced any of that.*" There in that sentiment lay the intent of God. We must be willing to hear what God is saying (see Matthew 11:15). We don't have to experience evil to know the value of good.

My prayer life (hearing God) now as it relates to my

leadership roles consists of more listening than speaking. I would say it is about 80/20. In this season, I have discovered it is more important to listen for God's input than give Him mine. I only want the knowledge He desires for me. Only the right knowledge employed rightly is power. What is the makeup of your prayer time?

So God can encourage us - Give a help meet

We were not wired to live and function alone. Anything we can accomplish by ourselves may not be the ultimate purpose of God for our lives; therefore we must develop healthy relationships. It is important to notice that Adam had no one on the earth in a body to have fellowship with. What do we do when there is no one available for fellowship and/or teamwork? We might not have the first option God had of just putting Adam to sleep and creating Eve from a rib (Genesis 2:21-23).

God in creating Eve gives us some powerful leadership concepts.

- If Eve was also created from the earth, she would be an independent creation and forging of a relationship with Adam may have been more difficult.

- Help meet is a helper with same value, not a lesser status, but a lesser function.

- Adam sees her as a part of him. Bone and flesh. Created out of him.

As leaders, we have options in developing teams. Here are two I employ. First, I develop those in my present circle with the understanding some may not journey with me through to the complete vision fulfilment. A portion of those among you will not be able to shift from their mindsets and embrace the systems and mandate given to you. This is why I am big on developing emerging leaders from within the ranks of those entering the kingdom through the Spirit directed efforts of your ministry. Your sons and daughters in the ministry are then rib helpers.

Second, at times I fill positions from without. Some are outsourced. An example is with the ministry's accounts. When entering a new assignment, I often place the responsibility of financial record keeping with a local CPA. The reasons for this are to model the importance of fiscal management and paint a clear picture of my motive of building the kingdom of God and not my personal empire.

I also, at times, look to fill key positions from without, hiring those who understand that their responsibility is to work themselves out of a job by developing their replacements. These precious saints are engaged knowing there are expected outcomes and timelines.

Finally, I am convinced that God provides the tools and relationships necessary for success. I have arrived at a place in my maturity process where I am grateful for those the Lord has surrounded around me. I endeavour celebrating their gifts and skill-sets with the same value as I put on mine. I view the godly assembling of a team as a blessing from God.

He encourages us by equipping us with the right team.

So that God can empower us - Give opportunities through a mandate

We have been given, among others things, a dominion mandate. Rule over the earth, not others. Every leader has something to manage.

As the moon reflects the light of the sun so are we to reflect the image and likenesses of our Creator God. This was the commission given to Adam and Eve. They were to reflect on earth heaven's brightness. The church has that same responsibility. We are godly reflectors.

As a teenager, among other things, we had a competition centered around who had the better bicycle reflectors. I can still visualize the assortments displayed every Saturday. Recently as I was pulling into my driveway and it was full of the grandchildren's and their friends' bicycles, it brought back many memories of the power and beauty of reflectors. We are His reflectors, full of power and beauty.

SCRIPTURE TO EXPLORE

Explain Psalm 51:10 as it may relate to God's intent in creation.

According to 2 Corinthians 5:17, what happens to those who are in Christ Jesus, and how do you think this changes one's priorities?

SCRIPTURE TO EXPLORE

Compare Proverbs 1:7 and Colossians 2:2-3. What do these verses have in common?

SCRIPTURE TO EXPLORE

Mark 6:7. What do you think was Christ's intent for sending
them out by twos?

_____

_____

_____

_____

_____

_____

_____

_____

_____

MY REFLECTION THOUGHTS

_____

_____

_____

_____

_____

_____

_____

_____

_____

_____

_____

Digging Deep

Employing the creative gifts given to us by God is a function of effective leadership. It is impossible to fulfill God's plan and purpose for our lives as it relates to leadership without using the attitudes He has given us. Our leadership roles present us with numerous opportunities in this area. Each stage or season of development as leaders may bring new issues that tend to cloud our thinking and hinder us in the area of creativity, but we must continue to grow as leaders. During your personal study time, look up the scriptural references for the following topics and complete the exercise. Discuss your findings with a friend. You may want to complete the entire exercise with a friend.

Mandates

1. Genesis 9:1

2. Matthew 28:19-20

3. Mark 10:42-45

a) Name three expected outcomes of biblical mandates from the above scriptures.

_____

_____

_____

_____

_____

_____

_____

_____

b) Name two biblical characters who fulfilled a mandate:

1. _____

2. _____

c) How have you responded to God-given mandates? Give an example.

_____

_____

_____

_____

_____

_____

_____

_____

_____

Leadership Teams

3. Exodus 18:17-23

4. Acts 6: 2-4

5. 1Corinthians 12:12-18

a) Why are effective leadership teams necessary for success?

b) Why do you think a leadership team is referred to as members of a human body?

c) List the three most important leadership positions in your ministry. Give reasons for your choices.

EVALUATE THE STEP

To evaluate means to look over or inspect and see the good and the bad in something. When we evaluate here, we attempt to discover how we should view the creating process in our leadership endeavors. In this evaluation process, you will briefly review some of the topics presented in Intend on Creating. This evaluation step is designed to assist you in confronting any hindrances that may have a grip on your life and are preventing you from properly using your leadership creativity in ministry.

CREATIVITY – NEW PREPECTIVE

Leadership creativity is finding a new way to do something. It's leading and approaching a task from a new perspective or angle. Creativity allows leaders to overcome seemingly impossible obstacles. Let's take a look at two examples

King Solomon

What was creative about the ruling? (1Kings3:16-28)

Nehemiah

How was this leader creative, and what did his creativity
secure? (Nehemiah 3:28-30)

PERSONAL DISCOVERY

• What concerns you the most about your leadership creativity skills?

• Which aspect of Intend on Creating is most difficult for you and why?

• Name three persons who you feel would give you godly advice in regard to this step. Make an appointment to see at least one and seek advice or steps to overcome that which most hinders your leadership creativity.

1.

2.

3.

PRACTICE THE STEP

As we learn and develop steps to success, it is important for us to walk in these steps. By practicing, they become a part of our everyday life and ministry. The step we have just studied is Intend on Creating. How can we practice this step? We practice it daily by evaluating our thoughts and actions. Conduct a daily personal inventory, allowing the Holy Spirit to search the inward parts, revealing what is in your heart.

As revelation comes, write down your personal adjustments. This will be accomplished over a period of time. We were created in God's image and gifted with among other qualities the ability to be creative as we walk in fellowship with our Creator and serve others.

YOUR PERSONAL ADJUSTMENTS

List ten adjustments that you will make to ensure you live and serve in the intended will of God as it applies to the concepts presented. Be specific.

1.
2.
3.
4.
5.
6.
7.
8.
9.
10.

Practice, Practice, Practice. It is important to practice this exercise of ten and continually make the necessary adjustments to ensure you continue developing in this area. God is interested in us having longevity in our personal lives and ministry endeavors. Practice this step to success, and maximize opportunities and manage challenges that flow into your life and ministry. Practice still makes perfect.

SEE THE SUCCESS

Success may be instant and progressive. True success is derived from facing the seasons of our lives God's way. Intend

on Creating sets the stage for a productive endeavor. I encourage you to observe others in ministry as they model the
concepts presented in this step. Don't be afraid to glean from
effective leaders. Creativity is part of a leader's lifeline. I
encourage you to follow through on further developing this
step in your personal life and leadership endeavors. You may
wish to develop the habit of keeping a journal. Document
your steps, pausing at times to reflect, readjust, and ready
yourself for future success. Practice the step, see the success.

State the Step

Every step God takes toward us is done on purpose for a purpose. He is an Intentional God in Seeking.

Teach the Step

Intend on Seeking

INTEND ON SEEKING

*And they heard the voice of the LORD God walking in
the garden in the cool of the day: and Adam and his
wife hid themselves from the presence of the LORD God
amongst the trees of the garden.*

(Genesis 3:8)

Our quoted Scripture shows an Intentional God walking as
He normally does toward Adam and Eve, this time to communicate through a series of questions and introduce through
an intentional act a plan of redemption.

I am thankful that missteps on our part do not cancel out
the God's intentional plan for us. He still shows up and has
a system for offering us an opportunity to repent and get
back on track. It is well thought out and unwavering. It is
intentional. We were created by an Intentional God.

What amazes me is that throughout the Bible are many
accounts of a God who shortens the distance between Him
and His creation. He in His infinite love comes looking for
us. His walk is intentional, and there are no missteps on His
part. May we leave the comfort and security of our places of
abode and worship and be as intentional with others as God
is with us. Let us be as committed as our Maker in providing
equipping, encouragement, and empowerment to others.

Our quoted Scripture implied that God visited His ultimate creation on a regular basis. Even when Adam and Eve disobeyed and were hiding, God still arrived not only on schedule, but with a commitment to commence the restoration process. One of the greatest challenges I have faced over the years has been developing the commitment to go look for the hiders.

There are a number of reasons why we shy away from reaching out to the hiders. For me, it was not just the potential uncomfortable feeling of confronting and, or being accused of being partially responsible for their absence, but also the concern for the welfare of those still in my care.

Often I pondered the possible negative ratifications of following the example set out in Matthew 18 verses 12-14. Are the ninety-nine mature enough to not wander away if I focus on the one? To feel secure in this principle, I shifted my ministry and leadership efforts to reflect the desired outcomes foreseen in Ephesians 4:11-13 namely:

As a leader, I must position the right gifts in leadership.

If we are to experience a high level of success, then we must position the right leaders in the right places within our organizations. Gifts out of place are wasted gifts or at best underutilized. Some years back, a dear friend asked me to assess his leaders and advise if they were positioned correctly.

After a few workshops, which among other tools included the use of spiritual gifts and temperament profiles, I presented my findings to the senior pastor. We discovered that some leaders where so committed to supporting their pastor that they had committed to ministry roles outside of their gifting, and this led to unproductivity or in some instances moral failure. The roles assigned, requested, and volunteered for were not perfectly fitting for their gifts and personalities; therefore the pressure was too much (see Matthew 11:28-30). God has a mission or assignment for each of us that fits us perfectly.

Leadership assignments where deemed necessary were adjusted and internal and external success followed.

I once heard it said that success is partly due to having the right people on the right bus in the right seats. What does the composition of your bus look like? The positive makeup of your bus in part enables you to be released to seek out the hiders.

As a leader, I must be committed to equipping.

What captures our attention secures our efforts. As a leader, it is easy and often common place to became sidetracked and focus on the less important elements of our leadership roles. One of the more important roles is that of equipping emerging leaders in our care. There is truly no success without a successor. This role must remain a high priority in our leadership practices.

Once the right gifts are positioned, it is vital to continue a system of equipping. We must always be improving on our acquired skill sets and creating opportunities for those we lead to do the same. A great portion of my time is intentionally invested in coaching and providing the necessary environments for emerging leaders to grow and develop.

One year as a family we released our bowl goldfish into our outside pond. We were amazed how they grew into the new environment. We had no idea they have the physical ability to develop their size. They were at least ten times their bowl environment size. It is vital that as a leader you create an environment for your team that provides the ingredients for growth. You may have no idea of the potential or capacity they possess.

As a leader, I must release the saints into ministry.

Similar to how we released the goldfish, you must be willing to release your team. Often it is through the releasing of the team into ministry that they reach their full capacity.

This process of releasing may take different forms. Here is one example. A few years back, our church was preparing for a mission trip to Cuba. The process of securing religious visas is a drawn-out one, but we were successful in the endeavour and shortly after I sensed the Lord was forbidding Shena and me from traveling. I felt impressed to turn the leadership of the trip over to one of our ministers who had left Cuba as a youth in search of a better life. We released him into this ministry appointment.

It was a Spirit-Led Leadership Step, and this precious brother was ushered by the Spirit and a supportive team into a new level of effectiveness for the Kingdom of God. We must not be afraid to release those equipped into meaningful ministry. Give them opportunities to grow measurably into their environment. Every trip to Cuba we marvel at the favour and increased ministry he is experiencing. His passion for ministry has intensified and a healthy attitude of purpose ownership has immerged; however, you very well know that not all releasing is this successful.

However the alternative of not releasing those ready for ministry into their purposes may produce splits, confusion, and delay in development. Obedience is always our responsibly as leaders, and outcomes God's.

As a leader, I must strive for unity in and of the faith.

Unity is paramount for obtaining and maintaining ministry success. Without unity, roles will never be given an opportunity to flourish, and assignments opportunities to be fulfilled.

We can agree on a course of action without unity of belief, but how successful do you think that is in the long run? How can we minister together without agreement? (see Amos 3:3) Unity of the faith speaks clearly about oneness. As the human body works in oneness when healthy, so does the church. As a pastor, I understand the perfecting of the saints is a team effort and accomplishment. We must draw on the other gifts given to the church.

God-given power and authority is often visible in organizations and ministries that demonstrate unity (see Acts 2:1).

As a leader, I must want the fullness of Christ realized.

The fullness of Christ cannot be realized in the Believer's life here on earth, yet we must strive for it. As long as we are pilgrims on a journey in this world, we are to commit ourselves to spiritual growth.

This spiritual principle as well holds true for leadership development. It has been said that leadership is a journey and not a destination; therefore we must be committed to obtaining ongoing growth levels as leaders. We never arrive to a perfect stature in leadership development; however like the fullness of Christ, what we obtain needs to reflect a commitment to excellence. We must pursue fullness in our spiritual as well as leadership endeavours. This ought to be intentional.

It is still a work in progress, but we are experiencing small steps toward fulfilment. We have committed ourselves as ministry leaders to continually practice the above, and we are experiencing growing success. This success has allowed us to minister in an *out-of-the building way.* A few years ago, we embraced a new motto for our church: "*Committed to Our Community*," not just the Community of Faith, but the entire community. We are better prepared now to visit the hiders in the cool of the day.

In Adam and Eve's failure the eternal intentional thoughtfulness of God as it relates to redemption is observed. Ultimately where the First Adam failed, the Second Adam restores. Jesus Christ restored man to a place to fulfil the intended will of God (see I Corinthians 15:45).

Bridge to Next Intend

In man's failure, redemption is revealed by two intentional acts of God.

- God clothed Adam and Eve (Genesis 3:21)

- God protected Adam and Eve (Genesis 3:22-24)

In the above Scriptures, we observe compassion in action. Provision for nakedness and a measure of protection are provided. What allows this? Is it simply the love God has for His creation, or something else added to the mix? There are varying responses we have when we are disappointed with others. The varying in our responses are, in part, due to our differing tolerance levels, but more so I believe because of our preparation levels. God is so intentional and focused on keeping the main thing the main thing that before mankind was even created, He had a plan for redemption. Jesus Christ slain before the foundations of the world (Revelation 13:8). The Blood of Jesus Christ was shed in the intentional thoughts of God even before it was necessary. How amazing the love and thoughts of God are toward us. As parents, we try to anticipate the needs of our children and provide an assortment of insurance plans. As leaders, we do forecasting to determine courses of action. These are the results of our love, responsibly, and commitment for those in our care. Jesus encourages us to extend that circle of commitment (see Matthew 25:42-45). He attached measurable acts to love:

- Feed the hungry

- Provide for the thirsty

- Show hospitality to the stranger

- Cover the naked

- Visit the shut-ins

I intend on living out my God-given reflected image and likeness, do you? If unsure where to begin in your community efforts, I encourage you to start with the compassion ministries listed by Jesus.

God is so thoughtful that He had a plan before our existence. He was prepared for our failure and restoration before we existed. Part of His plan may lead to Him locking you out of a place for your own safety. It is wise not to ask for something we know He has denied us. Adam and Eve were separated from the garden because of the tree of life. He did not want them to be permanently preserved in their sinful state. Like Lot's wife, the tree of life would have produced an eternal pillar of salt.

Our intentional planning should also include anticipated setbacks and provide a strategy for getting back on track. Remember, the greater the preparation, the smoother the execution. The one who listens keenly to the voice of the Spirit need not be caught off-guard, but rather sense each step of the way the impulses of his Creator. We are made in the image and likenesses of our Creator and have the ability through Him to tap into this Divine Quality of Intentional Planning.

SCRIPTURE TO EXPLORE

Explain Matthew 4:19 as it relates to hiders.

According to Luke 19:10, what was the purpose of Jesus coming to the earth and how is this accomplished today?

SCRIPTURE TO EXPLORE

Compare Matthew 7:7 and Psalm 34:4. What do these verses have in common?

SCRIPTURE TO EXPLORE

Acts1:8. Explain the importance of this verse as it relates to seeking out hiders.

MY REFLECTION THOUGHTS

Digging Deep

Intend on Seeking is a two-fold function of Christian leaders. First, as leaders we are to seek out the hiders - those who are purposely under the radar because of guilt and/or disobedience. Second, intentionally seeking out the right gifts and positioning them in the right roles within our organizations. It is impossible to fulfill God's plan and purpose for our lives as it relates to leadership without adequately addressing this two-fold function. Our leadership roles will present us with numerous opportunities in this area. Each stage or season of development as leaders may bring new issues that tend to cloud our thinking and hinder us in this two-fold area, but we must continue to improve our skill set. During your personal study time, look up the scriptural references for the following topics and complete the exercise. Discuss your findings with a friend. You may want to complete the entire exercise with a friend.

- **Gifts**

    1. 1 Peter 4:10-11

    2. 1 Corinthians 12:7-11

    3. Ephesians 2:10

a) List three gifts given and their functions.

b) Name two biblical characters who were faithful to their gifts:

    1.

    2.

c) What are the predominate gifts in your ministry? Give an example of how one is used.

- **Equipping**

    3. 2 Timothy 2:2

    4. 2 Kings 2:9

    5. Ephesians 6:11

a) Why is a teachable spirit important in leadership?

_____

_____

_____

_____

_____

b) Name a leader in the Bible who had a similar desire as Elisha. Fully describe the event.

_____

_____

_____

_____

_____

c) How does one put on the Whole Armor of God? Give an example from your personal life.

_____

_____

_____

_____

_____

EVALUATE THE STEP

To evaluate means to look over or inspect and see the good and the bad in something. When we evaluate here, we are attempting to discover how we should view this step and how we can improve in our Intend on Seeking. In this evaluation process, you will briefly review a few concepts presented.

This evaluation step is designed to assist you in confronting any hindrances that may have a grip on your life and are preventing you from properly seeking.

POSITIVE RELEASING

One of the more difficult yet rewarding acts of a Christian Leader is releasing others into ministry. Often this releasing is in one of two areas. At times we release someone within our organization to embrace ministry and leadership roles under the covering of our organization. At other times, we release them to function outside our direct oversight but under the overall covering we provide.

• Who calls the Believer and on what merit? Why do you think this is necessary? (2 Timothy 1:9)

- Please comment on the following Scriptures as they relate to releasing.

  - 1 Corinthians 7:17- 24

  - Matthew 28:19-20

- Luke 4: 17-19

- 1 Timothy 1:12

PERSONAL DISCOVERY

• What concerns you the most about releasing?

• Which aspect of Intend on Seeking is most difficult for you and why?

• Name three persons who you feel would give you godly advice in regard to this second step. Make an appointment to see at least one and seek advice or steps to overcome that which most hinders your Intend on Seeking.

1. _____

2. _____

3. _____

PRACTICE THE STEP

As we learn and develop steps to success, it is important for us to walk in these steps. By practicing, they become a part of our everyday life and ministry. The step we have just studied is the step *Intend on Seeking*. How can we practice this step? We practice it daily by evaluating our thoughts and actions. Conduct a daily personal inventory, allowing the Holy Spirit to search the inward parts, revealing what is in your heart. As revelation comes, write down your personal adjustments. This will be accomplished over a period of time.

YOUR PERSONAL ADJUSTMENTS

List ten adjustments that you will make to ensure you live an Intend on Seeking ministry lifestyle. Be specific.

1.
2.
3.
4.
5.
6.
7.
8.
9.
10.

Practice, Practice, Practice. It is important to practice this exercise of ten and continually make the necessary adjustments to ensure you continue developing Intend on Seeking efforts. God is interested in us having longevity in our personal lives and ministry endeavors. Practice this step to success, and maximize opportunities and manage challenges that flow into your life and ministry. Practice still makes perfect.

SEE THE SUCCESS

Success may be instant and progressive. True success is derived from facing the seasons of our lives God's way. Intend on Seeking is a life or ministry-long journey. It reflects the heart of our Creator for His creation.

The great commission as a commandment has Intend on Seeking as its core purpose and is directed to all Believers. It is expected that we will be seekers of the hiders and prepare others to respond to this God-given commission.

This mandate is not negotiable. I encourage you to observe others in ministry as they model this step. Don't be afraid to glean from effective leaders. I encourage you to follow through on further developing this step in your personal life and leadership endeavors. You may wish to develop the habit of keeping a journal. Document your steps, pausing at times to reflect, readjust, and ready yourself for future success. Practice the step, see the success.

State the Step

Every step God takes toward us is done on purpose for a purpose. He is an Intentional God in Restoring.

Teach the Step

Intend on Restoring

INTEND ON RESTORING

And he saith unto them, Be not affrighted: Ye seek Jesus of Nazareth, which was crucified: he is risen; he is not here: behold the place where they laid him. But go your way, tell his disciples and Peter that he goeth before you into Galilee: there shall ye see him, as he said unto you.
(Mark 16:6-7)

Jesus Christ the only begotten of the Father was intentional in all that He did on earth. On one occasion after His resurrection He explained to His disciples that His assignment was to do everything written or spoken about Him by inspiration of God (see Luke 24:44). We are encouraged to live as committed to God's purpose for our lives.

Many years ago, I was encouraged by a minister to discover or find myself in the Word of God and live out what it says. There are many biblical characters we may learn from and see traits of our roles in their stories. Their assignments may resemble ours and in this we draw wisdom from their walk. Apostle Paul encourages the church at Corinth to follow his example as he follows Christ's. (see 1 Corinthians 11:1)

The mirroring of Christ is a powerful aspect of the evolution process within a Christian leader's life. Are you able to make Apostle Paul's declaration to those you lead?

In this brief overview let us look at a few of Jesus's intentional acts in respect to His death and resurrection.

Jesus Christ was Intentional before the Crucifixion.
Matthew 26: 52-54 and John 18:11

- In the garden, He is betrayed and submits to it because of His commitment to fulfil His assignment.

- Jesus rebukes Peter for taking matters into his own hands, and restores the ear of the attacked solider.

So many advocate and teach that any form of suffering or hardship indicates that the Believer is outside of God's will. This assumption at times may deter the fulfilment of purpose. Often the road of our purpose-fulfilment journey is bumpy and causes a level of discomfort.

It is important for us to not use our God-given powers or abilities to circumvent the will of God for a season because of the discomfort it may bring. At times it requires more faith to walk through the fiery trial than look for a way of escape.

By faith we must believe that everything ordained by God for us is purposeful (Romans 8:28). No matter the assignments or challenges associated with our faith walk, in the end it will all work for the good for those journeying in God's intentional will for their lives.

I so appreciate the narratives in the Gospels of the interactions between Jesus and Peter. Every time Peter does something rash, Jesus is there to bring him back on track.

What encourages me is that the revelation of who Jesus was, was shown to Peter (Matthew 17:17). We often hear from God in our developmental stages of life and leadership. Yes, leadership is a process and not a destination, with interactions with God along the way.

It is my desire to be as committed to developing those the Lord has surrounded me with as Jesus was with Peter. It is so important for us to see the potential in others regardless of their present circumstances. I believe when the Lord looked at Peter He saw not only potential but great capacity.

Jesus Christ was Intentional with Peter and the Disciples.

Luke chapter 22:31-32 indicates the enemy of our soul asked for permission to sift Peter and the disciples as wheat. It is interesting that the response of Peter is: I am ready to go where ever you go. It becomes clear that Peter understood the proposed shifting was to do with cancelling out intentional living. Yet even though he understood the intent of the enemy, he still failed. Has this ever happened to you?

Jesus quickly answers: "You will fail. But I have prayed for you and when you are converted or renewed. When you are back on good footing having recovered from your fall, and then strengthen your brothers."

The purpose of God for our restoration always seems to be two-fold. He restores us so we can fulfil His will for our lives, which is first to live out the likeness and image we were created in. Second, He restores us to be in position to minister and strengthen others. Here in this recorded text Jesus shares it, and also in the Psalms we hear the heart of David (Psalm 51:10–15). Create in me a clean heart and renew a right spirit in me. Lord if you do this I will teach transgressors your ways.

We see in these two accounts the purpose of God as it relates to relationships. Live right with God and empower others. Jesus when asked which commandments we should keep, rolls all into two. The two are our vertical relationship with God and our horizontal with others.

Jesus Christ was Intentional after the Crucifixion.

At the empty tomb, Jesus leaves instructions. The angel is to tell the disciples and Peter that Jesus is risen and on an assignment to meet them (Mark 17:7). Peter had failed the Lord, but the intent of God is restoration.

Some years back while attending a leadership conference, I notice a gentleman alone at a ministry booth. I instantly recognized this once prominent clergyman. As the expression goes, he had fallen from grace. I have never quite accepted that phrase, but it is a common one that means he messed up big time, and everyone knew it.

I noticed other leaders were avoiding him like a plague. I struck up an interesting conversation with him and listened to his restoration story. He acknowledged his assignment from the Lord had shifted mainly because of the lack of acceptance by others, but that in his restoring, the Lord had carved out a niche for him and that he was eternally grateful to the Lord for His grace and mercy. Restoration is an intentional action of our Creator God, and must have a place in our ministry endeavours.

To restore is to return something to its original design and purpose. The Second Adam restores us. Sometimes we are guilty of thinking our restoration is to be to the greatest point in our fallen state. This is shortsighted, and God restores us to His original intent for us before the fall. Through the power of the cross, He invites us to walk out this divine purpose. I have learned that God's view is often different than mine.(Isaiah 55:8) My views have at times been connected to my experiences, which fuel my expectations, and often these expectations are inferior to God's.

Lately I have been looking into the Bible, searching especially for God's original intent for mankind. We are better equipped to face the challenges of life and ministry when we are sure of God's original intent for us. This knowledge provides for us a sure foundation or base to live and lead from.

Have you ever been guilty of praying, Lord if it's your will? This has happened to me on occasions when reviewing opportunities to serve our community. I have adapted my thinking process to focus on keeping at the forefront God's intentional will for mankind, and the resources of our faith community as two of the determining factors in what our response will be.

The last major determining factor is to ascertain if this is part of the stretching process for our growth as a ministry.

This factor is the more intense one, simply because it often involves our leadership team, physical space, and finances.

The instructions and mandates we receive at the empty tombs of our lives and ministries are very important. Observe the following from Christ's empty tomb:

1. He was not there but left a communicator.

2. He left clear instructions, which were communicated.

3. He encouraged the disciples and singled out the apparent future leader.

4. He restores to fulfil the original intent of God.

Let us INTEND on always creating, seeking, and restoring God's way!

SCRIPTURE TO EXPLORE

Explain Luke 23:33 as it may relate to a role of a Christian leader.

According to Psalm 34:20, not one of Jesus's bones would be broken. What do you think is the significance of this as it relates to restoring?

SCRIPTURE TO EXPLORE

Compare Galatians 6:14 and 1 Corinthians 5:7. What do these verses have in common as it relates to the crucifixion?

Psalm 23:3. Why do you think restores precedes leads? What do you think is the importance of this as it pertains to leadership?

Digging Deep

Intend on Restoring is a mandate and privilege given to Christian leaders. It is impossible to fulfill God's plan and purpose for our lives as it relates to leadership without ministering restoration.

Our leadership roles will present us with numerous opportunities in this area. Each stage or season of development as leaders may bring new issues that tend to cloud our thinking and hinder us in the area of biblical restoration, but we must continue to serve others in this area. During your personal study time, look up the scriptural references for the following topics and complete the exercise. Discuss your findings with a friend. You may want to complete the entire exercise with a friend.

- **Restore**

    1. Galatians 6:1

    2. Psalm 51:12

    3. 2 Corinthians 13:9

a) What should be the manner in which one restores another?

b) Name two biblical characters who had a ministry of restoring:

1. _____

2. _____

c) What did David hope restoration would provide? Give one example of your desired outcome for personal or ministry restoration.

_____

_____

_____

_____

_____

_____

_____

_____

EVALUATE THE STEP

To evaluate means to look over or inspect and see the good and the bad in something. When we evaluate here, we are attempting to discover how we should view Intend on Restoring. In this evaluation process, you will briefly review a few concepts on restoring. This evaluation step is designed to assist you in confronting any hindrances that may have a grip on your life and are preventing you from properly enquiring of God.

RECONCILIATION

The purpose in part of the work on the cross was to restore us to right fellowship with our Creator, and to give Believers the ministry of reconciliation. Let's take a closer look at this ministry.

• Explain the importance of this Scripture as it relates to restoring. (2 Corinthians 5:18-20)

PERSONAL DISCOVERY

• What concerns you the most about the ministry of reconciliation?

• Which aspect of restoring is most difficult for you and why?

• Name three persons who you feel would give you godly advice in regard to this third step. Make an appointment to see at least one and seek advice or steps to overcome that which most hinders your ministry in this area.

   1.

   2.

   3.

PRACTICE THE STEP

As we learn and develop steps to success, it is important for us to walk in these steps. By practicing, they become a part of our everyday life and ministry. The step we have just studied is Intend on Restoring. How can we practice this step? We practice it daily by evaluating our thoughts and actions. Conduct a daily personal inventory, allowing the Holy Spirit to search the inward parts, revealing what is in your heart. As revelation comes, write down your personal adjustments. This will be accomplished over a period of time.

YOUR PERSONAL ADJUSTMENTS

List ten adjustments that you will make to ensure you live a restoring life style. Be specific.

1. _____
2. _____
3. _____
4. _____
5. _____
6. _____
7. _____
8. _____
9. _____
10. _____

Practice, Practice, Practice. It is important to practice this exercise of ten and continually make the necessary adjustments to ensure you continue developing in your restoring efforts. God is interested in us having longevity in our personal lives and ministry endeavors. Practice this step to success and maximize opportunities and manage challenges that flow into your life and ministry. Practice still makes perfect.

SEE THE SUCCESS

Success may be instant and progressive. True success is derived from facing the seasons of our lives God's way. Restoring of God sets the stage for a productive endeavor. I encourage you to observe others in ministry as they model a restoring lifestyle of Jesus Christ. Don't be afraid to glean from effective leaders. Restoring is a leader's lifeline. I encourage you to follow through on further developing this step in your personal life and leadership endeavors. You may wish to develop the habit of keeping a journal. Document your steps, pausing at times to reflect, readjust, and ready yourself for future success. Practice the step, see the success.

PART TWO

Intend Leadership Personal Audit

INTEND LEADERSHIP PERSONAL AUDIT

Please read each of the following statements. Circle the number that best describes how true each statement is of you.

CREATING

1. I am committed to always lead from my Godgiven image.

   1. True

   2. More true than false

   3. More false than true

   4. False

2. Consistent and effective communication with my core team is a leadership trait that I consciously try to practice.

   1. True

   2. More true than false

   3. More false than true

   4. False

3. I always share prudent information with my core leaders, and always ensure they know the ground rules.

   1. True

   2. More true than false

   3. More false than true

   4. False

4. As an organization, we committed to developing leaders from within (bone and flesh).

   1. True

   2. More true than false

   3. More false than true

   4. False

5. I understand and function in my Kingdom Mandate.

   1. True

   2. More true than false

   3. More false than true

   4. False

SEEKING

1. I approach my rebuilding process in a similar fashion as Nehemiah.

   1. True

   2. More true than false

   3. More false than true

   4. False

2. I understand the value of worker safety and always implement sound measures.

   1. True

   2. More true than false

   3. More false than true

   4. False

3. I always take steps to maintain unity among my work teams.

   1. True

   2. More true than false

   3. More false than true

   4. False

4. I always wait patiently on God's direction in my readjusting efforts.

  1. True

  2. More true than false

  3. More false than true

  4. False

5. I have a firm grip on principles for overcoming discouragement.

  1. True

  2. More true than false

  3. More false than true

  4. False

RESTORING

1. I am committed to the ministry goals regardless of the difficulty of the process.

    1. True

    2. More true than false

    3. More false than true

    4. False

2. I always clearly communicate my intent on restoring fallen leadership within our ranks.

    1. True

    2. More true than false

    3. More false than true

    4. False

3. I always take personal responsibility for my part in the ministry of reconciliation.

    1. True

    2. More true than false

    3. More false than true

    4. False

4. I always welcome the input of my team as it relates to the process of restoration.

1. True

2. More true than false

3. More false than true

4. False

5. I have my teams' necessary commitment level to lead others in the ministry of reconciliation.

1. True

2. More true than false

3. More false than true

4. False

TOTAL YOUR SCORE

Total the numbers and place them in the spaces provided then multiply them by the given number.

True = 1
More true than false = 2
More false than true = 3
False = 4

True _____
More true than false _____
More false than true _____
False _____

Add the numbers together and read the results of your audit.

Total _____

IF YOUR TOTAL SCORE IS

15-25 The three INTEND STEPS are engrained in your personal life and leadership role.

26-35 You are practicing the three steps. If your total score is closer to 35, you need to pay more attention to one or more of the steps.

36-45 You need to continue to work on developing all three steps.

46-60 Others probably do not view you as an effective leader. You may want to take some time to rethink your motives for service.

PERSONAL IMPROVEMENT STEPS

The purpose of this exercise is to focus on identifying areas that need improvement and developing a plan for the same.

STEP ONE: List an area where your score is a 3 or 4.

CREATING

My score is a _____

STEP TWO: Develop a plan for personal improvement.
Refer to your personal adjustments list of ten to draw your information for developing the plan.
Refine your list of ten into five and record it here.

PERSONAL DEVELOPMENT PLAN

1.

2.

3.

4.

_____

_____

_____

_____

_____

_____

_____

_____

_____

_____

_____

_____

_____

_____

_____

_____

_____

_____

_____

_____

_____

_____

_____

5.

PERSONAL IMPROVEMENT STEPS

The purpose of this exercise is to focus on identifying areas that need improvement and develop a plan for the same.

STEP ONE: List an area where your score is a 3 or 4.

SEEKING

_____

_____

_____

_____

_____

_____

My score is a _____

STEP TWO: Develop a plan for personal improvement.
Refer to your personal adjustments list of ten to draw your information for developing the plan.
Refine your list of ten into five and record it here.

PERSONAL DEVELOPMENT PLAN

1.

2.

3.

4.

5.

PERSONAL IMPROVEMENT STEPS

The purpose of this exercise is to focus on identifying areas that need improvement and develop a plan for the same.

STEP ONE: List an area where your score is a 3 or 4.

RESTORING

My score is a _____

STEP TWO: Develop a plan for personal improvement. Refer to your personal adjustments list of ten to draw your information for developing the plan. Refine your list of ten into five and record it here.

PERSONAL DEVELOPMENT PLAN

1.

2.

3.

4.

5.

You have now completed your personal development plan. As you begin to implement your plan it will be wise to continually review and seek guidance from the Holy Spirit. Your plan will assist you in moving forward in your walk in the Spirit. It is important to strengthen your weak areas and build upon your strengths. This process may be repeated as necessary.

HOPE Initiative — How it Works!

Vision

By 2030, our vision is to accomplish the following: (1) Drastically reduce poverty in targeted areas of the Bahamas and the Dominican Republic. (2) Provide ways and means for sustainable self-stability for individuals, families, and communities. (3) Develop emerging biblical servant leaders and social entrepreneurs for ongoing community development and transformation.

Mission

Phase One of our vision is to empower the underprivileged to break the cycle of poverty and apathy through the vehicles of economics and biblical leadership, training, and mentoring. This not only transforms individuals and families but complete communities.

Unique Value Proposition

Our CTC Network USA programs give individuals, families, and communities opportunities to embrace a hand-up and not simply another short lived hand-out. Our initiatives help restore dignity by uniting communities through commerce, education, and social development programs. We take our programs not only to urban areas, but also rural and often remote communities rich in human and natural resources, which gives hope for real change in the present and well into the future.

Ministry Background

The CTC Network USA is a non-profit 501(c)3 organization that provides consulting, training, and coaching services to community leaders and individuals throughout North America and the Caribbean. The CTC Network USA has offices in three nations.

Business Model and Strategy

Put simply, CTC is executing a two-phase strategy:

- Provide micro-credit programs.

- Develop a sustainable agricultural/live-stock model business in each targeted nation.

Products and Services

Fully equipped Enterprise and Biblical Leadership Development Centers (HOPE Centers). Youth Preparedness Programs, and retail products from model businesses.

How To Support Jonathan and Shena Carey, founders of The CTC Network, serve throughout the Caribbean focusing on:

- HOPE Initiative

- Short-Term Mission Trips

- Salt and Light Conferences

- 5R Circle Weekends

World Outreach serves as their home-base office. They serve administratively in many ways, handling mailing lists and online donor relations. World Outreach allows Jonathan and Shena to focus on their mission of developing leaders and transforming communities in the Bahamas and the Caribbean.

For Tax Deductible Gifts:

1. Online Donations for our account –

www.WorldOutreach.org

Click Donate and select Jonathan and Shena Carey #76
(USA and International Cards accepted)

2. Or, Mail Checks to –

World Outreach Ministries

P.O. Box B Marietta, GA 30061 USA

(designate for Jonathan and Shena Carey #76)

95638517R00061

Made in the USA
Columbia, SC
20 May 2018